R 19 15.

MW01251837

Grown

&

Sexy

- 40 Life Lessons Every Woman Should Be Aware Of -

Charmaine 'Macka Diamond' Munroe

Co-Author Klyf Antonio

Published by PageTurnER Publishing House
7 Sunset Road, Passage Fort, St. Catherine. Jamaica W.I,
Email: pageturnerja@gmail.com

Copyright © 2010 by PageTurnER Publishing House

ISBN 987-1-4276-4853-2

REGISTERED TRADEMARK

Cover Design: Karl *Cliff* Larmond
Edited By: Ingrid Abrahams
Photo Editing: KLJ Photography

Grown & Sexy
First Printing 2011

Dedicated To
The Progressiveness of ALL Women...
UNIVERSALLY

WE ARE ALL GOD'S GIFT...to Men...

Macka Diamond

3

Grown & Sexy

Contents

Grown & Sexy

Preface

Charmaine Alvaree Munroe; that is the name you will find on my birth certificate, passport, driver's license, house deeds, and any other relevant legal document that I possess, but most know me simply as Macka Diamond.

For those who already know what they are about to read, consider it a reminder, and for those who don't know me, well allow me to introduce myself, I am one of Jamaica's most dynamic and stellar Dancehall recording Artistes; who, regardless what anyone says and regardless what you have heard, it simply cannot be denied that over the years, I have solidified myself as one of Reggae/Dancehall music's luminaries.

Variety is the spice of life, and we are all entitled to our opinions, so I am quite aware that not everyone is going to like me, and not all fans of Reggae/Dancehall music are my fans or will be my fans, but be that what it is, my track record is also what it is; and my accomplishments are undeniable, and to top all that, I must also add that I take pride in the fact that I have not only survived, but thrived over the years in an industry that is both male dominated and egotistical – an industry known worldwide as Dancehall.

Yea, Macka is forty, but please add still relevant after that, because that is also what it is, *still relevant*, an accomplishment within itself if you ask me, but whether you agree or disagree, the facts are just that - facts, and for me to be here, still doing what I do, the evidence is clear; I must be doing something right.

I know some may be wondering, what does Macka have to say again, she already wrote two books, did the acting thing, and gi wi (gave us) one bag a hit tunes, so what now?

Well to answer your question, writing a book of this nature was the last thing on my mind, I was actually playing with *Bun Him Again,* which was going to be the follow up to *Bun Him,* (the novel) but that was put on pause after I kept finding myself being bombarded with questions from young ladies who now seem to realize that Macka has way more to say besides what they hear at parties or on the radio.

So that's what this is all about, not just another novel, but a book aimed at addressing a few feminine issues from my humble prospective that I realize are vital and universal in scope.

I am not trying to be a guru or act like I have some type of degree in human psychology of any sort, but what I have is experience and experience teaches wisdom, and in real everyday life, that can be worth much more than any degree; regardless of the institution that awards it.

That's what this book is all about, clearing up speculations and assumptions, while also sharing some of what I have learned over the years. This book is not an effort to gloat about or over what I have done, like becoming Dancehall's first author, penning what is now dubbed, Jamaica's First Dancehall Novel, the both famous and infamous, *Bun Him!!!* Which was named after my monster hit single of the same name; and this is not about what I experienced while dabbling in acting; playing the lead role in the Caribbean action thriller, *Redemption of Paradise*.

No, this isn't about any of that, this is about the other stuff, because besides the on stage antics, media reports, witty lyrical prose, rumors and speculations, the truth is, there is much more to me than being the woman that has made the moniker, '*Money-O*', famous.

Bottom-line to this book:

The aim of this book is to advice whom it may, while also creating conversations that will lead to positive developments, because if that's all this book does, then I would have accomplished that which I set out to achieve. This book is about life, mine, yours, because there are some things that every woman simply must know by the time she is at a certain age if she is to excel to her true God given potential; so we are all involved in one way or the other. That is the unadulterated fact, and the sad part about life is that none of these things are taught in our schools, private, tertiary or any other institution for that matter, but life demands that we know them or be overwhelmed by them.

It not only sounds sad, it is, but such is life, and none of us are exempt from the demands and expectations it brings, and it makes no difference how prepared we are or aren't…Like most females I learned some things early and some I learned late, some I learned the hard way, and there are some that I'm actually still trying to learn, but even with that I still feel it's imperative and appropriate that I share some of what I have learnt, what I view as some of the most critical factors to be considered by everyone of us who desire to be more than just the next head turner or, the girl next door.

This is what *Grown & Sexy* is all about, sharing a little of what I have learnt from experience and life in general; a little of what I believe every young lady needs to be aware of before she gets swept away by the manipulative tides of life; tides which are always there, regardless if one is aware of them or not, tides which also give no regard to class, race, nationality, education, accomplishments, family background or popularity.

Note: *Grown, actually has little to do with age - & - Sexy, has way more elements to it besides the body.*

BIO:

If ever there was a female born to be an Entertainer, then without doubt, Macka Diamond would be her name. A female who from her early years of youthful yearning, literally and practically breathed and lived the desire to become the entertainer that the world now knows and hails as one of Dancehall's stalwarts...Over the years a lot has been said about her, written about her, reported about her, rumored about her, and even propagandized about and around her, but is there any truth to what has already been said, and if not, what is the truth about one of the few women of Dancehall, who have been able to not only show up, but show up and show out, on the male dominated and at times even egotistical and chauvinistic stage - that is now known world over as - Dancehall?

Charmaine Munroe, now known to the world as Macka Diamond, was born in Kingston, Jamaica on January 12, 1971. She spent her early years in the Tower Hill community and later grew up in the Sunshine City of Portmore, Saint Catherine, located on the outskirts of Jamaica's capital. She attended Holy Childhood High

School; an all-girl Catholic School in Kingston, one of the city's most prestigious learning institutions, but even then it seemed as if her focus was more on becoming an entertainer, opposed to excelling academically.

Then again, who could blame her, when the influence of music was around her from an early age? Charmaine's father is Phillip Munroe, a record producer from the golden era of the Late Great Reggae Pioneer, King Tubby's. With her father working closely with future legends such as the Late Great Gregory Isaacs aka The Cool Ruler, Cornel Campbell and The Crown Prince of Reggae himself, Dennis Emmanuel Brown, the influence of the drum and bass was constant.

BUT...

It was after hearing Artiste's such as Sister Nancy (aka Mumma Nancy, a female deejay, and Dancehall trailblazer), that she was convinced that she too was going to make the desires of her heart a reality; Charmaine was going to become a deejay.

With her father already being involved in the music industry, the interest she showed in music was understandable, but her mother wasn't so sure about such a career move. Number one, she was a girl, and not many females were involved, so it was only natural that her mom was concerned, especially with all the violence that was known to plague the Waterhouse community where most of the studios were located at the time; places that Charmaine would eventually have to visit should she indeed become what she desired. The violence in and around the surrounding areas at the time was so rampant that it became the biggest contributor to the family's relocation to Portmore St. Catherine – Waterford to be specific. The concern of Charmaine's mother was understandable, and so was the desire she had for her daughter, who she thought would have stuck to a more traditional career choice, but to the disappointment of both her mother and teachers, Macka's decision became official upon completing High School in 1987, when she decided against any further academic pursuit and instead, started knocking, kicking and shouting, at every studio entrance that she became familiar with.

The determination that drives Charmaine Munroe 'Macka Diamond', today is not new, but has been with her from the very beginning, because not only did she make up her mind and stick to it, she was independent in her pursuit.

We all know the age old rule; that we use all the connections we have to get where we are trying to get, but instead of using her father's connections to get her foot in the door, Macka decided to do it alone. In retrospect her approach may've been innocent, but it was what it was; she wanted in, so she decided to go to someone who was already in.

Her name was Lady Junie, and as simple as it may sound, Macka asked a friend to show her where Lady Junie, {a happening foundation female deejay at the time} lived; and just like that she went and introduced herself, and the rest like they say, is history.

Maybe it was destiny, or maybe Junie was just intrigued by this little girl's boldness, but whatever the reason was, Lady Junie was not slow to realize Charmaine's potential, and she soon began to take her protégé around, introducing her to some of the movers and shakers in the music industry.

We live what we learn and often emulate what we see, and Charmaine was no different, listening to all the female artistes who were big at the time, and drawing from influences from the likes of Mumma Nancy (centre), Lady Ann (right), Lady G (left) and her own personal tutor of sorts, Lady Junie (previous page).

It's all in the name...

At first, Charmaine had decided on Lady Charm being her stage name, but after she had made her first record, (an answer to then popular Major Mackerel hit 'Don Ban'), the producer insisted that the song be released under the name, Lady Mackerel.

Needless to say, but Charmaine did not like such a development one bit, but in her desire to get her voice heard on wax, she wont along to get along, all the time confident that her time would come and she would eventually make it under her own terms.

'Don Girl,' the title of Charmaine's first recording, proved to be the hit she had hoped it would be, and with that came more opened doors, allowing her to record for legendary sound system owners and producers such as the Immortal Stone Love, and the legendary King Tubby's Kingston 11 label.

With new recordings under her belt, Charmaine's voice was soon heard all over, even in various combinations with those already considered Dancehall staples; and with that achieved, the young sensation was soon seen creating havoc every time she was introduced to a stage, or called around a sound system.

With time came growth, and with growth came responsibilities, and one such responsibility that came with being involved in the industry of Charmaine's choice, was that it took way more work than she had imagined; constant sleepless nights, but not even that seemed to faze her. She soon became known as a workaholic, going toe to toe and blow to blow with her male co-workers, a stance that she has maintained over the years; a time span in which she has developed a style and an on stage persona that is now reviled by many with similar job descriptions.

As time would have it, Charmaine eventually became a stalwart and dependable feature on Kingston's bubbling dancehall scene, but even then she was not satisfied, she was still in preparation-mode, building and preparing for her big break, which as popular as she was getting at the time, she still viewed as fleeting.

Just like today, Dancehall has always been male dominated, and with women a new addition to the Dancehall environ *back then*, the women were more times than not treated like second class citizens, but come what may, Charmaine was not about to give up her dreams – the fight was on.

The setbacks were many, and the hurdles seemed to get higher every time she cleared one; *but when the going gets tough, the tough gets going.* Charmaine was not the first young, starry-eyed female who had decided to try her hand at the male dominated craft, and she was sure she wasn't going to be the last, but what separated her was her determination. What doesn't kill you only makes you stronger, and she had obviously learned that along the way; allowing her obstacles to serve as motivators (to try even harder), instead of the agents of discouragements that they should have been.

"When I could not get a tune to play on the radio that was hurtful, even when I recorded a tune that I know was good it did not get played," remembers Macka of her early years in the music industry. "A lot has changed, but a lot still remains the same," continues Macka, "females still have a hard time getting their work heard today, pretty much like back in the day – but the way I look at it is, if this is what you want, then fight for it, it's that simple."

Sometimes a change is good:

After years of mediocre success, Charmaine decided that she had finally outgrown her Lady Mackerel epithet in 2003, and decided on a name change that led to Macka Diamond; and along with the new name came a different, more aggressive lyrical approach.

That year Vybz Kartel's massive hit 'Tek Buddy' had put forward the theory that women were after pots and pans in return for sex, an opinion that Macka Diamond was not in agreement with, so much that she came hard with the counteraction/reply, entitled, 'Tek Con'. Macka's ribald reply got the message across, as she informed Vybz Kartel (and misogynists everywhere) that women were after way more than plasma televisions and other material trinkets!

"The change can come if all female artists decide to get more serious, get aggressive like the males, because Dancehall is what it is, a bit aggressive at times," states Macka, whose hard work finally paid off in the summer of

17

2004 when *'Dun A Ready'* topped the Jamaican charts; *the first time a female had topped the charts in the last four years – an accomplishment within itself at the time!*

Wickerman & Captain Barkey

'Dun A Ready,' Macka's unapologetic swing at men who failed to meet the required bedroom standard, touched the nerves of many men, while connecting deep with the female Dancehall audience who had grown tired of Dancehall's relentless boast of stamina and machismo.

Queen Paula

FINALLY - Someone was telling a different side to the story: a side that was not usually mentioned in 'polite company'. The effect of *'Dun A Ready,'* was so great that it even touched the nerves of some of the Island's top male deejays, but like all things before, Macka was also able to address that situation amicably.

"I got a lot of flak from men everywhere about that song, it was as if they felt like I was talking about them directly, like I knew of their shortcomings," jokes Macka, "I even got attitude from some of the male deejays about the song, and some of the selectors didn't even want to play it, but hey, next time I will know who can take a joke, and who can't."

Macka and fans in St. Kitts

Over the years Macka Diamond has had to make some difficult artistic decisions in order to make it to the point where she finds herself today. She has gone through name and style changes, worked alone or with partners such as Queen Paula and in collectives such as Captain Barkey's Worm Dem Crew.

Contrary to what many may believe, with over twenty years of working non-stop in the male dominated environment of Kingston's Dancehall scene; Macka Diamond could never be described as an overnight sensation. Her measured delivery and unbridled humour, or as she likes to put it, *just saying what others are thinking,* has gained her legions of fans all over the world, but even with all that, performing for Macka remains an intimate affair as she approaches each stage as

BlackER & Macka

though it was her first chance to make a lasting impression; a *modus operandi* that has worked like a charm.

Like change, sometimes a little controversy can also be good, and in 2004, Macka again proved that to be true with the release of the comical and controversial *Bun Him*, a monster hit song in collaboration with Dancehall brother, BlackER, formally known as Blacker Ranks, which not only encouraged women to cheat if their lover wasn't acting right, but it went on to even give a little advice which added insult to injury; taking all she can while making her exit.

This song not only solidified Macka's position among Dancehall luminaries, but also created a ripple effect of controversy across the island and the Dancehall worldwide, upon its release, and still to date, woes audiences and remains one of those urban hot-button topics in Dancehall circles.

Constantly in demand for shows and recordings, Macka Diamond has overcome a lot to be finally calling her own shots, an accomplishment she achieved with the emergence of her own Entertainment Company; Diamond District Ja.

With these accomplishments safely tucked away under her

Bun Him Book Launch

belt, and now legitimately one of Jamaica's leading and premier female Entertainers, Macka took her artistry to another level in 2007, with the release of her debut dancehall novel; Jamaica's First Dancehall Novel, entitled *BUN HIM,* loosely based on her mega hit single of the same name.

Bun Him the novel was a hit out of the gate, and went on to became the number one selling novel in Jamaica in 2007, and is still highly sought after worldwide to date. To the pleasure of her fans Macka Diamond again went

Macka & Winford Willimas - On Stage

against the grain, with the release of her sophomore novel; *The Real Gangster's Wife,* in February of 2010, again to great fanfare.

In addition to Dancehall and now literary success, Macka Diamond has also managed to achieve crossover success in the soca arena, copping a hit single with Patrice Roberts (from Machel Montano's camp) with the remix for the number one soca single *'Wukking Up* in 08.' In addition to this achievement, Macka has also collaborated with other soca heavyweights such as Faye-Ann Lyons (Wife of Soca Giant; Bunjie Garlin) and the vivacious Denise Belfont.

Macka Diamond's career has taken her far and wide, and from humble beginnlngs, this Dancehall Artiste has elevated from the days where she couldn't even touch the microphone freely, which soon turned into fighting over the microphone, to now performing on stages such as the coveted New York's Madison Square Gardens (a feat yet to be achieved by another female Dancehall Artiste), Hasley Crawford Stadium in Trinidad, the world famous Reggae Sumfest

Macka & Patrice Roberts - Reggae Sumfest 2008

and Jamaica's greatest one night Dancehall show, Sting, just to name a few. Macka has even extended her repertoire of accomplishments to include acting; starring in the 2009 full length Caribbean Movie, Redemption of Paradise, and even appearing on the popular Jamaican soap-opera, Royal Palm Estates.

A workaholic by nature, Macka has kept her shoulders to the wheel since even before, but more so after her new name-new attitude resurgence in 2003. Many would've probably thrown in the towel long before that and moved on, but not Macka Diamond, and thank God she didn't, because the evidence is clear; hard work does pay off. Macka has scored a list of monster hits, which include *Tek Con, Bun Him, Dun Aready, Hoola Hoop, Lexus an Benz, Dandy Shandy, Robbery* and *Tink Bout Mi*, in addition to working with some of the best that Reggae music and Dancehall has cultivated, from the likes of the legendary Toots Hibbert, right down to some of Dancehall's hottest producers of the day; individuals that include the likes of Steven Di Genius McGregor, Christopher Burch, Don Corleon, and platinum Dancehall producer, Cordel 'Skatta' Burrell.

In addition to all that, this versatile female Entertainer, Author and Actress, who is also responsible for making the moniker, *'Money-O'* famous, has walked away with one of Reggae/Dancehall Music's most coveted awards: Female DJ of the Year; on not one, but three occasions, back-to-back, not to mention numerous other awards that include IRAWMA, Jamaica Observer Teenage Choice Awards and a variety of other music awards from various entities aimed at acknowledging the accomplishments of those who have committed themselves to the journey of Reggae/Dancehall music.

MACKA: "Claude McKay once said that the heights of great men reached and kept, were not attained by sudden flight, but they while their companions slept, were toiling upwards through the night. I learned that while in high school and it has stayed with me since, and it's pretty much one of the principles that I live by."

And with that said, and her track record being what it is, there is little denying that the sky just may not be the limit for Charmaine *Macka Diamond* Munroe; her sights may just be set way higher.

Money – O...

Macka Speaks :- On...

MONEY - FAMILY - FRIENDSHIP - RELATIONSHIPS
THE ENTERTAINMENT INDUSTRY - AGE & SEX

Ask most men in Jamaica what they think about Macka Diamond and you will hear something to the tune of: *"Macka, who she, she love too much money star."*

Yes, that is the general consensus of most Jamaican men when asked about Macka Diamond; they like her, there is little doubt about that, but most feel as if she is out of their financial league, and are always quick to point out her blatant verbal romance with the coveted piece of paper she is always talking about. The women on the other hand simply love Macka's talk of financial empowerment, but to every coin lies two sides, and Macka's take on the matter is night and day when compared to what is perceived as the general focus of most woman's cry, which always seem to revolve around the currency of choice; the almighty dollar.

"It's not a matter of loving money, but to be real, it's a matter of loving what money can do, it's that simply, every woman want to dress up and look good, every woman wants to live good, eat good, drive good, and make sure her children are taken care of and provided for. As great as love may be, it takes money to do all that, not just love, and if a man is with a woman and really means her well, then I don't see anything wrong with him taking care of her financially, not just physically," states Macka, without apology.

MACKA CONTINUES: "This is how I view it…I am just saying what a lot of women are already thinking, they are just not saying it, but believe me, they are thinking it. And let's face some other facts; because if I weren't saying what the ladies wanted to hear or want to say, then my fan base would not be as large as it is worldwide."

Macka and dancers, Reggae Sumfest 08

"Money-O"

"In Jamaica and in a lot of other parts of the world, there is a perception that a woman who asks a man for money or is after a man's money is a gold-digger, and if that's all she is after, then that's true, but on the flip side of the coin, ask yourself this question, what is the man after?…Let's be real here,

25

because most men are only after sex, sure it may lead to other things, eventually, but sex is always at the top of their priority list, and that is his prerogative, so what is wrong with money being on the top of a woman's priority list?"

PEOPLE ARE ALWAYS GOING TO TALK: "People are always going to talk, that's just life, if you do good, they're

going to talk, and if you do bad, it's going to be the same, and above all that, there is no human being who has ever, or who will ever be able to please everyone, I know that, so I don't even attempt to do it anymore."

"People are always going to be people, and people have minds of their own, and that allows them the privilege of forming opinions. We are all different, so it's only natural that our opinions differ. I talk about what I feel is important to me in my music, some people like it and some don't, but such is life, not everyone likes Bounty, they say he talks too much about guns, and he's always too cross, angry and miserable, but he still has a huge fan base, regardless who talks or who doesn't. "Beenie is the same too, but the

BEENIE MAN

doctor is still performing surgery. Dem talk all type a things about Lady Saw along the way, so much that they even banned her from certain shows at one time. The story is the same with Kartel and Mavado, but the same was also true with Shabba, Super Cat, Ninja Man and a whole lot of other entertainers; remember when Admiral Bailey did do *'two year old?'"* People talk about the good the bad and the indifferent, so I don't pay too much attention to it,

VYBZ KARTEL

because who was talked about more than Michael

Jackson?....People are still talking about him even now, so what does that tell you?....That tells me that people are always going to talk, regardless of who you are or what you do, especially if you are a public figure....Listen, people talk about Jesus, and it's not all good, so that should say it all. I talk about money and some people don't like it, but as long as some do, that topic will always be dear to my heart."

"Which woman doesn't have a dear spot in their heart for money?" asks Macka, answering her own question with the words, "let's be real, we live in a society where everything cost money, there are light bills, mortgages, and water bills, plus gas prices are constantly on the rise, as much as we love our children, they cost an arm and a leg, food prices are always going up, and the list goes on and on, so if we are to

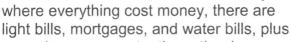

be fair, the society we live in demands money, and a lot of it too, so I don't see what the big deal is about me talking about money; and to top all that, if I were saying something that was more to the benefit of the men, like something more sexual or domestic, then the issue would be something else, or maybe I would be considered a Dancehall darling then. I don't know, but I feel as if money is not just important, but very important, so let's put ego aside and be real."

ON BEING THE MONEY GODDESS: "The whole money goddess thing seemed as if it was in the making from way back in the day, from even before the whole money costume thing, because I was saying money-o way before that, but the whole money goddess thing didn't come to life until we were in one of the islands and Cool Face, (producer, songwriter and DJ) started playing around with it and introduced me as the money goddess, and it just stuck. It was that simple."

"I don't feel as if I love money more than any other woman, I may just be more vocal about my desires, or seem more vocal because I have a platform, but I believe that most women have unrepressed desires when it comes to finances and comfort, they just don't talk about it openly, but regardless what some may say or not say, truth is, I am not talking about anything that is not relevant or on point; money is vital, and it takes more than *stamina* and other *sexual prowess* to fulfill the needs of a woman...and men need fi know dat."

On Family:

FAMILY: "I grew up knowing both my parents, living with both of them at one point, and I am still very close to both of them until this very day, so that's my foundation, and I don't stray far from that."

"I am not antl family, I believe family is important, and is an institution that should be nurtured. Our society today does not promote too much of that, and sometimes circumstances don't always allow things to work as they are suppose to, but that still doesn't take away from the fact that family is the foundation and should be nurtured."

Macka and son in Canada

29

Macka cuts cake with son - Birthday party - Canada

"Being an entertainer, I have come to realize the importance of family in more ways than one, because with me always on the road, travelling here and there constantly, I have become very dependent on family; for example, my son lives with my mother in Canada, most of the times it is my brother who does the driving for me, and when I'm on the road, it's either my sister or my father who keeps an eye on my home and properties, so yes, family is very important to me, because if I didn't have them, then I would be under way more pressure than I am at times."

Macka and Dad, Phillip Munroe - Teenage Observer Awards '08

"I am the third of six children that I know about. I have three brothers and two sisters, and we all get along fine. It's not like we have this fairytale brother and sister relationship, but we're good, and we are always there for each other constantly, in any way that's possible; for example, I have a brother who is a police officer, and when I'm having my birthday bash or parties, trust me, I can always depend on him to show up and monitor things for me, regardless how many other people are already in place for security purposes."

Macka watches while her son feeds grandma - Birthday party - Canada

On Friendship:

"Dem sey good fren bettah dan pocket money, and believe me, that is true, because over the years friends have proven to be even more vital than money at times."

Queen Paula, Lady G and Macka

"I am not an anti social person by a long shot, anyone who knows me know that I'm very approachable, but at the same time, I am not going to lie to you and say that I am the friendliest person on the planet, because life has thought me to be very careful of

Beenie Man and Macka - Airborne

those who I allow to get too close, so to be very honest, my real friends are few, but they are solid."

"For example, people like Lady G and Queen Paula have been my friends for years. Lady G was even instrumental in my resurgence on the Dancehall scene, being one of the first producers to voice me as Macka Diamond on her *G-String* label."

"I have friends outside of the industry, real good friends, like Diamond, a friend of mine who lives in New York, the same

Diamond who I also took the name *Diamond* from, then I have friends who are like sisters to me, like Pinky, Dahlia, Latisha, Sandra, trust me, names too many to mention, but they are there, and they all know themselves. However, with me being in the industry so long, it seems as if most of my

Captain Barkey and Macka

real friends are in the industry also; and when I say friends I want it to be clear, I am cool with almost everyone, but when it comes to being friends that's a totally different situation. I am not just talking about someone you just know last year, or know because of the industry and you say this is your friend, no, I am talking about friends that I have known for over a decade and are still good with, regardless what we have been through, or regardless how long ago we have, or have not seen each other; people like D'Angel, Captain Barkey, Capleton, Beenie Man, Black-ER, Teflon, Bounty Killer, just to name a few, are some of those in the industry who I consider my friends; why, because of where

we are coming from and what we have been through over the years. Bounty for example was one of the first artistes to voice me and Queen Paula on his label; Priceless, not to mention looking out for us over the years by giving us constant dubplates so we could sell to sound-man

Macka and Oneil from Voicemail - RIP

and make a money when nutten nah gwaan back in the day, trus mi, a nuff time Killa put my pot a fire."

"Oneil from Voicemail was also a very good friend of mine; he was one of those who was always encouraging, always able to bring a smile to my face, just a genuinely nice person."

"I also find that a lot of my friends are men, don't ask me why, but that's just the way it is, so much that one of my best friends, Teflon, was the one who was responsible for writing *Bun Him*, my most successful commercial hit single to date."

"I did a song not so long ago, which said *my friends dem come from dolly house and lastic* (rubber bands), in other words, if we good, we good for the long haul. Change is good, but sometimes it's best to stick to the evil that you know."

Teflon (songwriter) and Macka

"Some people bun new friend, well not me, because if it's never new, how is it going to get old?...So that nuh mek too much sense to me. It's just a matter of who the person is, what they are about as a person and what their motive is when it comes to you. As long as that is clear and you are comfortable with it, then you're supposed to be good."

"No friendship is perfect, this is life, and life alone comes with give and take, sometimes more taking than giving and vice-versa, and when it comes to friendships, these things are mandatory, because we are human beings and we have different ways, views, opinions, tendencies, attitudes and motives, so although we mesh, we will never mesh one hundred percent, and that can put a strain on any friendship, at any time, if the parties involved aren't willing to give and take - take the good with the bad."

"Queen Paula is one of my best friends, but we still clashed at Sting one year; a clash that was so serious that we didn't talk for a while after that, but we are still friends, today we're good, so after the hype and ego thing simmer, we good again. Black-ER and I argue all the time, but after every storm there is a calm. To me, if a friendship cannot survive tests and trials, then it nuh good, it fragile, *warning sign*, handle with care."

"Like technology, always evolving, people are the same, always learning, trying and adapting, all the time evolving into something that he or she wasn't yesterday, that's just how it is, so it's natural to be cautious, because what you know or expect just might change without warning to your surprise, but at the same time, no man or woman is an island, so we all need people, and not just family or intimate relationships either. All that is good and needed, but we all need those casual, no strings attached, platonic relationships, and the sex of the person in which we find this makes no difference whatsoever, as long as the friendship is genuine, that's all that really matters."

'Friendship, always a two way street, sometimes even a six lane highway, but never a one way.'

On Relationships:

"Again, like friendship, this is a delicate subject, because although an affair between a man and woman is the first thing that comes to mind when one hears the word relationship, the truth is, relationships go way beyond that, and are actually more about non-intimacy, opposed to intimacy."

Is Macka in a relationship?

"I know that's going to be the first question on some people's minds, so let me answer - Yes I have a man, I am in a very understanding and nurturing relationship, but let's be real about this, because there is way more to relationships besides intimacy. I mean, take Shane Brown for example, (Juke Boxx Records) he and I have a very good relationship, but we are not intimate, look at me and BlackER, me and Captain Barkey, me and Capleton, and that's just four examples, and  the list goes on, and I know I am not alone either, because we all have a whole bunch of relationships with the opposite sex that are not intimate, but they are still relationships."

"Friendship is friendship, and can also be considered a type of relationship, but even with bringing that into the mix, again it proves the reality that we have all types of other relationships that are not intimate, so we can't just discuss the topic on one level, because the levels are multiple."

"Being in the music industry, a lot depends on relationships, *[and again, when I say relationship here, I am talking non intimate]*....Anyway, things can get real tricky if you don't get along with individuals in certain positions, and it's pretty much the same in any other industry, location on the map making no difference whatsoever – that's just the way life is. This however can be good and bad, with the bad being, it can get personal, it shouldn't, but it does, and this can lead to a whole lot of bias and side taking.....Let me explain. Sometimes it gets so personal in the industry that certain Disc Jocks and Selectors won't even play certain artistes songs, and that decision won't be based on how bad the song is; it's just based on a bias that comes from a certain relationship. So the whole relationship factor in the music industry is vital, because it can either make you or break you at times...And let's not forget for one second that this type of practice is not found only in music either, this is found in every industry, this is just life in general...we all tend to deal with those a little better with whom we have a better relationship, and most times it has nothing to do with sex or anything intimate...So let's be clear on that."

"What many fail to realize is that the journey of life itself actually encourages unity, encourages relationships, because we all need the help of someone else at some time or the other, and this is achieved with far greater ease if there is the foundation of a relationship to either stand on or build on. Let's say there is a hurricane, and your house got damaged, (and this is a true story from hurricane Ivan) if you don't have a good relationship with those you live amongst, you might be the last one to get checked on, and that could mean the difference between life and death. But had the relationship been good with those around you, believe me, after the storm passes, you may be one of the first persons on the minds of your neighbours, which is exactly what happened to me, so that alone goes to show the importance of relationships outside of intimacy. And it wasn't because of any Macka Diamond hype either; people just check for those who they are good with…it might come as a shock, but a little pleasant greeting here and there works wonders."

On the intimate side of relationships:

"On the intimate side of things my tendency is to go slow. Life has taught me well, so I take matters of the heart both seriously and slowly. I don't believe in running around, and although I may sing a song like *Bun Him*, I am not one that promotes, encourages or is involved in any sort of promiscuous behaviour, regardless what you may have heard or read. If I am in a relationship, I am in it for the long haul. I believe in being loyal to my partner. My work takes me all over the world and I meet all type of handsome and sexy men, and most have money…nuff money, and yes they come on to me, but I have to be a professional and not mix business with pleasure…*Oil and water* – not a good mixture."

"Presently I am not with the father of my son, simply because not every man can handle their woman being in the spotlight, and it eventually became a problem, especially with me travelling so often and working mostly at nights, but what am I suppose to do?…This is what I do, and he knew that before we got involved. It wasn't a matter of trust or anything like that; it was more a matter of being insecure. Men go through it all the time with their women, especially if they look good or are of a certain status, and women go through the same thing too, that shouldn't be the case, but like it or not, it is the reality"

"I believe trust is the main ingredient for any relationship to really work, but at the same time, each party has to be comfortable with themselves and each other for it to really work, because without that level of understanding, believe me, problems are going to arise."

"I don't want this to sound like an entertainer problem either, because this is a universal one, it is just what it is, women who are doing their thing tend to be a threat to some men, and that is one of the reasons why I move slowly, because it will be all good at first, but like old time people use to say, *'si mi and come live wid mi, a two different thing'* (to see me and to live with me is two totally different things) – in other words, what you see, isn't always what you get…A sad reality but one experienced all too often by too many women."

"I am not saying all men are bad, so please don't quote me wrong, because not for one second do I believe that all men are bad, because that is simply not so. Not all men are dogs, there are still a bunch of good men out there, most of them are just involved with someone else [laugh]. Men have faults, there is no denying that, but so do women, but in the same breath, I am a woman, so I speak from a woman's prospective first, and this is just one of those realities that almost all women know of personally, or know of in some way, shape or form; men will act nice at first, and some do remain nice, but some change, at times rather too quickly, and that alone is reason for caution. So yes, I encourage commitment, but I encourage cautious commitment. That's how I live my life and that's my advice to anyone, male or female."

Fashion and trends may change, but relationships should not be discarded or treated like last year's fashion, or some trend that is suddenly not so trendy anymore.

39

On The Music/Entertainment Industry:

"Wow, this is the big one...Where do I start?...Well, the music industry is what it is, very exciting, lots of glitz and glam, lots of attention, some of it unwanted at times, with probably the biggest thing of all being, unknown to the general public, what is presumed or believed to be a certain way at times, is not really what it appears to be."

"I know many people may not believe that, or even understand what I am saying, because this is not Hollywood, but a lot of it is make belief; some of it just isn't real, and isn't what it's presumed to be. It may seem to be all fun and games, but the music industry is a very complex entity, always changing, and extremely difficult, not to mention coming with a whole lot of

CUTTY RANKS

disappointments; and then to top all that, it has changed so much over the years, even coming with a dark side that once wasn't there…believe me, a lot has changed, so much that it's hard for even us as artistes to keep up at times."

"Let me explain, because people see it but don't really understand how it works. When it comes to being in the music industry as an entertainer on stage, an entertainer whose livelihood depends on making hit records, it's way different opposed to any other career choice, because the on-the-job training is constant. With any other career choice, where you learn a certain skill, enter that industry and put what you have learnt to work, although the music industry is similar in some ways, in others it's way different. How and why? Because it works off the vibe of the times and the vibe of the people, it's not contained or limited to one set formula, unlike a doctor who deals with broken bones, and the formula is basically the same wherever he practices. Not so with the performing part of the industry. In theory it sounds good, but it fails when it comes to practical, because you cannot use the same formula that you

use at let's say a Bar-B-Q, and expect it to work at a festival in Europe or at a park show in Miami or New York; trust me,

41

it does not work. The same formula that works for the show in the garrison will not, or may not work for the show in Virginia or Canada, but the doctor from any one of those places can do the same surgery, the same way, in any one of those places and the end result is going to be the same, unlike Dancehall, which calls for a tailor-made approach for each audience, so that alone is what makes this industry extremely tricky."

Tiger

"There are songs that I don't even perform in Jamaica, but I have to perform them in the islands; then there is Europe, where they call for both a different set of songs and at times a way different set, when it comes to performance. The formula is always different for almost every audience,

and that alone makes keeping up, [remaining relevant] that much harder, because keep in mind, you can be relevant here, but no one is listening to you anywhere else, and that can limit things to hype and no substance, a big factor that is presently plaguing the industry."

"One time when you were hot in Jamaica you were hot everywhere Reggae or Dancehall music was being played. When Tiger, Cutty Ranks, Shabba and Super Cat were hot, dem did hot globally, not hot in Jamaica and no one knew them in California, Japan, Zurich or Birmingham, but today it's different, why?...Not just because of the Internet, that's part of the problem, but another part is that today we have Reggae and Dancehall artistes popping up all over the world, and they are dominating their region, so with that, what has happened is that the focus on what's coming out of Jamaica has shifted, because our audience is being divided without us even realizing it – some songs still get through to the masses, but some never even get heard outside of an artiste's region, with the market place being the way it is - so like it or not, what has happened is that you can be hot in Jamaica and nowhere else, or it can be the other way around, which is a very common atrocity these days; some songs grow wings and fly out, and some have visa issues."

"A next thing that the average person may not realize is the pace at which the industry is moving. Right now a song or rhythm is hot for only one month on average, and it has to be exceptional to last longer than that and have any real impact. It's not like back when Half Pint did 'Greetings,' or when Tiger did songs like 'Wanga Gut' and 'Puppy Love.' Those songs didn't just last a month or two; they lasted way longer than that. Some people will say that those songs were just good and relevant to the times, and that is true, but good and relevant songs are still being made today, but the problem is,

The Legendary King Tubby

43

things have changed so much with downloads, CD burning and the Internet at large. Then there's so much music coming out constantly, the public is bombarded, and it gets hard to keep up, and some of the real good material gets overshadowed in the process, but it's not that there is no good and lasting work being done, it's being done every day, sometimes it just doesn't get the time to shine."

"In one way such a development *[the volume of music that is coming out and the pace at which it is coming]* could be seen as a good thing, but on the flip side of the coin, it can also be considered as bad and undermining, so it's like a blessing and a curse at the same time, because although we now have the ability to mass produce Reggae and Dancehall music, it also comes with drawbacks."

"I remember back in the day, there weren't so many studios around; there weren't even so many sounds and DJs, back in the day everybody was at Arrows or Jammys. At one time the Waterhouse area was almost totally responsible for Dancehall music, but now everybody has a laptop, everybody knows how to use ProTools, [A computer software now used in recording studios worldwide] and just like that they are producers; and the same goes for the DJs, because now everybody can download virtual DJ, learn to use the program, and the next thing you know, they have a pouch [cases used by present day DJs to carry CDs], and they are DJ This or DJ That, and the same goes for producers too, because suddenly everybody have a hot rhythm."

"Don't get me wrong, because this is not an effort to belittle anybody's effort or love for music, because that is what it is, and some are actually good, and at the same time, they are all making an effort to promote Reggae and Dancehall music, but on the flip side of all that, *let's be real,* some aren't that good, and some aren't promoting, they are actually demoting the thing, but depend on who they are, who they know, and what they have to offer, or where they are from, or whose brother, sister, cousin or son or daughter a person is, the next thing you know they have made alliances with industry movers and shakers and are being touted as the next big thing, when some of them weren't even worthy to begin with."

Too many cooks spoil the pot.

"Listen, dem sey everybody can dance but is not everybody is a dancer, and the same goes for DJs and producers too, because anybody can pick up a microphone or slide in a CD, but none of that makes you a DJ or Disc Jock, and the same is true for production, because we might like music, or have an idea about what something should sound like, but that does not make us producers, and it doesn't matter how well you can use ProTools either – **REMINDER:** Production Is actually called production for a reason, and it's about way more than splicing and sampling – Producers also do more than just produce, they *Create* – Creation borrows from little or borrows from none -

Music: More than technology and hype.

"I feel like one of the biggest problems facing the industry is that too many individuals are getting involved in the industry without the proper grooming, and getting involved for the wrong reasons."

"My thing wasn't to come into the industry to make a bag a money; it was more about expressing myself, being heard, because I felt as if I had something to say. Back then it wasn't about money because there wasn't any money to be made like that. Today all that has changed and many are entering the industry with a preconceived notion that simple

does not encourage creativity, instead it encourages compromise and mediocrity, and the music suffers or is sacrificed for some quick dollars and some here today, gone tomorrow hype, that cable TV and the Internet have tricked so many into believing is reality."

King Yellowman

"If you are not a real singer or DJ, but you go into the studio and record, and then you do the whole auto-tune thing, which sounds good as a finished production, and it becomes a hit with the people, what happens when that same artiste has to perform and there is no auto-tune, no ProTools to tweak the voice just right?...What happens then? It's a recipe for

disaster, but a reality that cannot be denied, because it happens every day."

Music didn't start with me, you or them.

"I get a lot of love from almost everyone in the industry, both locally and abroad, but at the same time it's not all love, because when it comes to the new kids on the block, at times they act as if we [seasoned contenders] are intruding on the very industry which we have been a part of for most of our lives, when if it hadn't been for the technologies of the new

Nadine Sutherland

millennium, all some of them would be doing for and in the

industry, is sit at home and listen, or go party to what they couldn't be apart of in the capacity that they can now find themselves in. They better thank God for technology…And oh, then there are the veterans who feel as if I shouldn't be this relevant today, shouldn't be this current, and all because their situation and mine are like night and day; so I get it from both sides of the fence, a lot of love, with what I like to call a steady dosage of hate."

"One of the oldest tricks in the book is divide and rule, and the music is suffering from that big time, because there is a separation between those who have been in the industry and those who have just entered it. Sometimes it gets so crazy, even some of the young artistes, Disc Jocks and

Producers start to act as if before them there was nothing, and after them it will be no more, so it has become somewhat of a clique and friend thing of sorts in some cases, and in the process, real talent gets stifled for what I call *Hobby Music*, because that's all a lot of it is, something to do while they figure out their next move in life."

"It's like everyone has forgotten that Reggae and Dancehall is actually bigger than any one or crew of us, because this thing did done set from way back when, but so many seem to have forgotten where this thing is really coming from, and act as if a dem invent it, ignoring the fact that before them there was a Yellow Man, before them there was a Barry G, before them was a big bad sound named Silver Hawk, there was

Gemini, there was Rory and Cancer from Stone Love, way before Chris Diamond and Geefus. There was Glamour Wayne, Inspector Willie and Stereo Graph, with Jose and Charlie, and then there was also Stitchie and Stereo One, with Wolfman, Daddy Blue, Ricky Stereo and all them other yute, and then there was Papa San and Creation. Who did big like San one time?...A him responsible fi Lady G, and let's not forget his brother either, Dirtsman and nuff more artiste who all came along and added a strength to the thing. What about Pinchers, Ninja Man, Professor Nuts, Little John, Burro Banton, Johnny P, Peter Metro, General Trees, Hammer Mouth, Early B, Nitty Gritty, Tenor Saw and the list goes on and on? What about all the females, like Dawn Penn, Mumma Nancy, Patra, Lady Ann, Lady Junie, Lady G, Junie Ranks, Sister Charmaine, Foxy Brown, Crystal – who had the big bad *'Twice my age'* with Shabba, what about Nadine *'Action'*

Sutherland and all the other females who paved the way?"

"The Thing bigger than any one, or crew of us, some of us need to remember that."

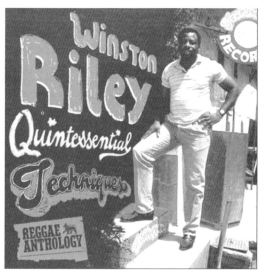

"The public may not know or may not have noticed, but behind the scenes this industry has gotten so weird, it's actually hilarious at times; young producers record young artistes, and avoid veterans because they claim they are setting a new thing. Young artistes avoid veteran producers, claiming they are this or that, most times based solely on what they heard from someone else, but as bad as that is, it gets even worse, with them [veteran producers] quickly written off as old school in many cases by young artistes, who seem to have totally forgotten that these were the same producers who produced hits like *this, that* and *those*; regardless of what is said about their other dealings. And then there are the Disc Jocks, who are mostly from the new school, so they play what they grew up on, and what they associate with, regardless if it's good music or not. So like it or not, the guard

GENTLEMAN

has changed, but this is one of the changes that can be for the worst, because if we are not careful, in a few years, Reggae and Dancehall may be a thing of the past, replaced by this fusion of everything else that we have allowed to influence our ideas and vibe, our lifestyle, our culture and even more rapidly than gradually; our music."

The World still wants authentic Reggae and Dancehall music, not some hybrid of the original thing.

"I travel all over the world, and I have come to the realization that we are missing it big time, because what I have found is that although the music is going one way in Jamaica, it has remained the same way, the original way it was, in the wider world at large."

"In recent times most of our music is like a constant remix. It sounds like Reggae or Dancehall, but it has changed, and is now a fusion of hip hop and world music combined, with a Reggae or Dancehall baseline, but it's not authentic, and although it may sound good and we dance to it, that is not what the world knows us for, wants or expects from us, they still want the authentic thing, and that is why artistes like Gentleman work in Germany. Why?...He has that authentic

Lady Mackerel @ 17- Sting 1988

sound, that roots and culture sound that is truly Reggae, the type of Reggae that the wider world has known for way longer than the ages of most of those who are trying to change what they are blessed to have inherited."

"Forget the excuses, because this is actually simple; if you are a Reggae or Dancehall artiste, stick to that. Sure you can experiment, but stick to what's yours. We see rappers trying our style all the time, but they experiment, maybe on one or two tracks for an album, or a single, but they are not trying to be Reggae or Dancehall artistes, but so many of our artistes, both new and established, are literally trying to be what they are not, and ignoring what we are, by culture."

"I have been in this industry long enough to understand it to some extent, and there are still things that take me by surprise, because that's just how much it has changed. Take clashes for example; I performed in a four the hard way clash on Sting in 1988. I

Sister Charmaine - Sting 1988

was the youngest and the most inexperienced, I was seventeen at the time, it was me, Lady G, Sister Charmaine and Lady Junie, and we didn't disrespect each other, didn't take it to the gutter, it was about lyrics, nothing like what we see today, **[CHECK OUT CLIP ON YOUTUBE]** and that is one of the key reasons I don't even entertain such assignments. Papa San and Stitchie clashed and it wasn't like today, even the Ninja Man and Super Cat clash wasn't as bad as the ones of today. Today the whole clash thing is literally a matter of life and death, a far cry from where it used to be, just another example of how far we have come."

"It's just what it is I guess, like life, music is always changing. This minute we are into dance tunes, the next minute we are into social commentary, and before we even realize what's happening, we are into everything else that we really have no real angle on."

"I am not trying to be funny or make light of what is a serious issue, but if we are to be real, then we need to realize and admit that our music no longer seems to have an anchor, and that's why we stay drifting all over the place; playing with hip hop, R & B and everything else in-between."

51

"When Freddie McGregor topped the British charts with 'Just Don't Want To Be Lonely," he did it in authentic reggae style, not some crossover mix or fusion with Garage or some other English or European musical expression; - because that's all music is, an expression of a people's culture, and we seem to be forgetting ours with speed."

"Shabba Ranks attacked the world with Dancehall, and even when he did a song with KRS 1, Johnny Gill or Queen Latifah, he kept it authentic; listen to those songs now and you will see what I am talking about, and if we as individuals and as an industry, don't check ourselves, in a few years we might not have what we have become so used to and taken for granted; Reggae and Dancehall music."

"Remember sey Shabba did dun sey wi fi cool, cause U Roy dun rule, and U Roy a di teacher fi di dj school, and Charlie a did dun di principal from long time, so di ting cyaa change, it nuh fi change, unless is a different school wi a get wi degree dem from."

"There can be no denying that our music has strayed from its roots. The fun and wittiness gaan, remember General Degree and Professor Nuts, now the whole thing get serious and to survive, artistes are forced into compromising situations, because if you are not voicing certain songs, a producer don't even want to talk to you, and that dictates what is accepted and what is then fed to the public, and in recent times, it has not been too pretty, and that is one of the main contributors to the problems we have been experiencing in our industry - and the solution is simple, we have to get back to the basics."

"Back in the day we used to DJ around sound systems all night, and that's one of the things that separate the thing, because that was like constant practice, so we learned how to interact with the people and how to deliver our songs to an audience from early, so that killed stage fright and run weh di

The Late Great Nicodemus - performing on Stur-Mars - mid 80s

butterfly dem, but today it's different, what we have is a  whole bunch of recording artistes; studio DJs and a whole lot of auto-tune Singers, who are yet to master their craft, but who are at times representing the music on an international stage, which simply does not make any sense, because not only can't they represent the music, they cannot deliver to an audience that is outside of their everyday reality – unfamiliar territory – but don't ask them how the tour or show was – no, fisherman never sey him fish stink yet, check the reviews and reports outside of Jamaica yourself – it's not good. Now that does not mean they are not good as artistes, what it means is that they are just not ready yet, but at times they are being forced on the public under the guise of either finding or being the next big thing, which quite possibly could've been what the individual might have had the potential to become, if the room was given for them to develop and grow into their own. Instead we have Reggae and Dancehall mass production, where things look good, they even sound good, but they don't last - and this is  one of the main things that is messing up the music – well, besides hype and lack of artiste development."

Reggae and Dancehall big outta road, but we have to keep producing it, not some hybrid – to this day, who is bigger than Bob Marley? – And he never diluted or crossed over –

On Age:

"How old are you now?... Age…maybe this is the most interesting subject of all in recent times; at least when it comes to me, so let me dive right into it without hesitation, because this is so interesting and at the same time, so annoying, it's hilarious."

"I say that to say this, recently it seems as if there has been a deliberate attempt to push Macka out of entertainment, and an attempt not based on my ability to deliver or anything like that, but an attempt based solely on my age; and with that I ask, what is the retirement age in Dancehall or Reggae?"

Macka Diamond and Marcia Griffiths

"That is the question that needs to be addressed if there is a call for a person's retirement, because I have been in this industry for over twenty years and I have never been to a conference or heard any decision being made about the retirement age of Reggae or Dancehall artistes, but still there has been so much talk about who is too old for Dancehall and who isn't, who should retire and who shouldn't, especially me."

"I mean, can we be real here?...This is the industry I work in, we (Dancehall artistes) pay taxes, (at least I do) and we are a recognized body, this industry, like any other, contributes to the society, and every other industry has a retirement age, so what is Reggae and Dancehall's retirement age?...That is the million dollar question, and even if it were to be decided, I don't think it will be forty or anywhere near that, so I find this whole topic of age and retirement comical."

Macka Diamond @ St Kitts Music Festival

"Marcia Griffiths is one of the person's that I look up to in this industry in a major way, and she has been doing it from almost the beginning, and she is still doing it, still looking good, still have men drooling, so what, should she retire too?...And if someone should say yes, this is what I would ask them, why should she, when she is still able to do what she does, and do it well? So I laugh when I hear people say things like Macka is too old for Dancehall, and one bag a other tings, because the question still remains, what is too old for Dancehall, because agree or disagree, and as weird as it may be, this is one industry that does not have a set retirement age?"

"You know what, I think I will retire when I am not able to deliver, not able to do what I do effectively. Yea, I think I will retire then, when mi cyaa guh pon stage an wine and gwaan wid one bag a tings. Yea, I will retire then. So there, for all those who wanted to know when Macka is planning to retire, now you know."

"What else can I say?...I mean, it's not like I am not sought after, or I am getting booed off stages, or I am not making hits, Macka is Macka, check the record, check the radio station's play list, listen to the mix CDs, go to a party, all that speaks for itself, so I will leave that right where it is."

Hon. Portia Simpson Miller

"Like I say, this whole talk of age makes me smile, because the people who are saying this stuff are mainly the new comers to the industry, talking about who should retire and who shouldn't, as if someone died and left them the god of Dancehall and Reggae. But you know what I believe, it's a lack of self confidence on their part, because they feel like if we stick around then there will be no room for them, all the time not realizing that our fans are ours, and they have to now build their own, not call for us to get out the way so they can get a free ride."

"When I came into this industry, I didn't start a campaign for Mumma Nancy, Lady Ann, Lady G or Lady Junie to retire, no, I looked up to those who were there before me, and I came and made my own

Macka & Hon. Oliva Babsy Grange

fans, did my own thing, carved out my own niche, and that's

58

what it's all about, not all this talk about who should retire and who shouldn't, and at the same time, none of who are talking can fill the spot or spots, if they were to indeed become vacant."

President Obama and Audrey Marks

"I don't see anybody saying Portia (*Portia Simpson Miller- Leader of Jamaica's Opposition Party; PNP – and Jamaica's First Female Prime Minister*) or Babsy (*Olivia Babsy Grange – Jamaica's Minister of Youth, Sport & Culture*) should retire, and how old are they?...But it doesn't matter how old they are, because they are effective in their positions, and that goes for other females all over the world too, but let's keep it home for a minute, because females like Carlene Davis (previously Reggae Recording artiste, now a Gospel Recording artiste), Judy Mowatt (Reggae Recording artiste formally of Bob Marley's I Threes,

Paula Llewelynn

Sarah Palin

now a Gospel Recording artiste), Dorraine Samuels (Veteran Radio and Television personality), Audrey Marks (founder of Paymaster, Jamaica Limited, and now Jamaican Ambassador to the United States), Paula Llewelynn (the first woman to be appointed as Director of Public Prosecutions in Jamaica), are just some of the females in Jamaica who are in major positions of power, and none of these women are below forty, so what, should they retire, and give way to some young girls, who besides being

Judy Mowatt

young, literally don't have anything on or over any of these women?"

"Then there are the elder states women, the international females who simply cannot be overlooked; there is Oprah, Mary J Blige, Sarah Palin, Barbara Walters, Madonna and even Janet Jackson; none of these women are young girls, they didn't just turn twenty, but they haven't lost a step, they have actually gotten better if you ask me, so what, should we call for their retirement also? And I won't even talk about the men, because even with this issue there seems to be a double standard, because I don't hear anyone calling for any of them to retire, most of whose age might shock us if we were to actually see their Passports or Birth Certificates."

Carlene

"The way I see it, age is what it is, *a number*, and I may be forty, but I feel damn good! Grown and sexy, and funny enough, the men, both younger and older, all seem to be in agreement, so my issue with age is none. All I have to say to those who are calling for my retirement is; Macka is here,

Janet Jackson

this is where I work, and it's going to take way more than a few naysayers and a few haters to force me into retirement, because none a dem never hire mi, so none a dem cyaa fire mi!"

"Sometime people talk more than they reason, because if they were really reasoning, and have any real knowledge of how the world really works, then it would become clear

that Dancehall is so new in the bigger scheme of things, *unlike other genres of music,* that we haven't even had a lifespan that should have produced so many retirees; because I still see Bruce Springsteen [DOB September 23rd 1949] and Paul McCartney [DOB June 18th 1942] doing their thing in major, major ways, and they are both way older than some of our Reggae and Dancehall acts who are no longer active."

"I believe some of us as Jamaicans, (*I say Jamaicans because it's not a worldwide issue),* have a twisted and wrong way of looking at our industry and its players. If we take a look at other similar industries worldwide, it's totally different and the examples are numerous, but we don't even have to look too far to see that how we view age in the

BRUCE MAGIC
SPRINGSTEEN

Grace Jones

Lady Gaga

Jamaican entertainment industry is like night and day when compared to the wider world, because one big example is one a di real mumma dem inna di ting, right from over Spanish Town, Grace Jones."

"Just look at her, she has been doing it for years, from modeling, to music [Pull Up To My Bumper, My Jamaican Guy, etc.] to starring alongside Roger Moore [James Bond 007] in *A View to A Kill*, and she is still doing it on a major scale, and just for the record, she is sixty two years old, so what, should she retire?...Some might say yes, but why should she, when she is so relevant today (2010) that Puffy [P.Diddy] just did a collaboration with her on his Dirty Money - *Last Train to Paris* LP, and Lady Gaga, unknown to many, is a literal reincarnation of Grace Jones?...So in the same breath, as new and exciting as what is now seen is, nothing is really new, because everything that is, already was, created or invented by someone else, someone older, so who are we, you or me, to decide when a person should stop doing what they do, if they are still able to do it and do it effectively?"

Has JAMES BOND finally met his match?

ALBERT R. BROCCOLI Presents

ROGER MOORE

as IAN FLEMING'S

JAMES BOND 007

A VIEW TO A KILL

Starring TANYA ROBERTS · GRACE JONES · PATRICK MACNEE and CHRISTOPHER WALKEN
Music by JOHN BARRY
Production Designer PETER LAMONT
Associate Producer TOM PEVSNER
Produced by ALBERT R. BROCCOLI and MICHAEL G. WILSON
Directed by JOHN GLEN
Screenplay by RICHARD MAIBAUM and MICHAEL G. WILSON

United Artists

"I mean, the Commissioner of Police is not in his twenties, but he is still a crime fighter, and that does not take away from the younger officers. In other words, everybody has their role to play, and age makes little difference in certain cases, if we are to be real."

"And to be honest with you, it may be annoying, but this whole age thing is neither here nor there with me, because everything is suppose to get  better with time, due to experience and all the other elements, so why call for someone to retire when they are just improving?... And at the same time, if the older artistes should all retire, who is going to make music for their fans, or is it that music is going to have to become a medium that comes with a label that reads something to the tune of, *for the young only*, with them deciding what young actually is, and at the same time, controlled solely by them; the youth, so where does that leave older fans of Reggae and Dancehall?

"Hey, makes no sense to me, because from what I know, music is timeless, knows no age, focuses not on race, status or gender, it is just what it is, *music*, built by people, for people, and the last time I checked, we were still all people, age making no difference whatsoever."

Note: "Regardless what we think, feel or believe, time and countless futile efforts have proven that older people are not the best ones to make music for the young, but that doesn't mean you allow the young to just run off and do their thing...No, their efforts need to be supervised, but in the same breath, younger people are also not the best ones to

63

make music for those of a totally different generation, it is just that simple; the vibes and realities are night and day in comparison, but music is needed by all, old and young, and that leaves room for all artistes, age making no difference whatsoever."

"Fans grow old too, they wish they could stay forever young, but life always has a different plan….Forever young is a nice thought, but it doesn't work, so yes, fans do get old too, and they grow old with the same artistes that they grew to love over the years."

Michael Jackson was rehearsing for an extensive tour, and a tour that was already sold out, a feat that not many young artistes can do these days; he was fifty-one.

On Sex:

"Let's talk about sex...I guess we have to, huh, I mean, Salt-n-Pepa started this conversation from back in the day and we are still trying to wrap it up, so I guess it makes sense, especially since we live in such a sexed up society, where sex is weaved into almost everything from our commercials to our music. And oh, just for the record, there goes another Jamaican female who has done her thing in a major way and is still doing so beyond forty, Pepa from Salt-n-Pepa...Yes, Sandra Denton is Jamaican, she was born right here in Kingston, November 9th, 1969, which makes her how old?...Yea, but look at her, and after you do that, look at what she has done and is still doing. The girl is still

making music, she is an actress, an author and she even has her own reality show, after co-starring in the Salt-n-Pepa show, which was about the group as a whole, but let's get back to the topic at hand."

"Sex….Okay, where do we start?...First of all let me say it like this, sex is the next best thing to money if you ask me, it's just that good, but only if it's good sex, because not all sex is good sex, if you know what I mean."

"Anyway, let me continue by simply making it clear that every woman in her right mind should enjoy some good sex...Yes, from what I know and have heard, we all do, we may not voice it like men and brag of our sexual exploits, conquest or bedroom abilities, but we are into sex just like the men are. Some women may say that I am letting the puss out of the bag, but the puss done come outta di bag long time, so if my male friends are anything close to what they say they are, none of this should be news to them, but just in case they are not, take it from me, the same way you feel about sex gentlemen, or approach it, women are no different, we are just more subtle, a little more discreet, or to put it plainly, wi jus sneaking!... But trust me, as women we also have a thing or two to prove."

"And just for the record, let's not forget that General Degree did done let the puss outta di bag long time with, *'When I Hold You Tonight,'* because like he said, *'when man and woman go pon move, dem always have something to*

prove.'….It was so then, and it is still so today, but most men act as if is dem alone have something to prove, or as if women were just made for their pleasure only, and not them for ours also."

66

"I don't know where that foolishness came from, but for those men who didn't know, let me be the first to tell them, a nuh suh it guh, okay….sex is a Two-Way Street, but the vast majority of men seem to believe it's a One-Way, and that is one of the main reasons nuff a dem crash and lose out, and all end up a get bun; because dem have the ting twisted."

"Just ask any female who is willing to be honest, and believe me, the complaints will be many, because nuff a di man dem nah act right when it comes to their bedroom duties, but would bet dem life sey dem have di ting lock, when nothing could be further from the truth."

"And just for the record let me make this very clear, because I don't want this to come across like I am talking against the men, because I am not, because if they were to be honest, they would also admit that the situation is what it is. The ones who are good at what they do are good, but some of them need to get it right, because talk is cheap, and if something wasn't wrong, then the women would not be complaining, they would be lining up and taking numbers, but instead, a bear grumbling a gwaan – women talk!"

"And you know what makes this subject even funnier? This may sound a way, but I find that this is not just a local issue either, because would you believe that wherever I go, *Dun Already* is still received as if it's a new recording. Why is that so?...Maybe because of its relevance, I don't know, but maybe women are experiencing similar problems all over, so they can connect in one way or the other...And don't get it twisted either, because I am not the only female entertainer who has addressed this issue and gotten the same results, because so has Tanya Stephens *(Nuh Ready Fi This Yet)* and Ce'Cile *(Can You Handle The Wuk - done in collaboration with Sean Paul),* just to name a couple, so the

reality is obviously what it is, regardless what one man may say, the reality is, there is an issue that needs to addressed, if not with him, at least amongst his peers; because everywhere I go the cry is the same, women are complaining about dat little ting."

"I am no expert, okay, so don't get it twisted. Macka is no sex therapist, but I have ears, I hear things. I have friends, and I have had my own experiences, so I'm not speaking on this subject blindly. Some may not want to admit it but the truth is, a lot of our Jamaican men do not fully understand the art of sex, and what the whole sexual experience should be all about, because one of the main things that I believe needs to be understood, is that sexual satisfaction does not have to include pressure and pain, because for one, there is no such thing as sweet pain; pain is pain and pleasure is pleasure, night and day, just like how sweet is sweet and sour is sour."

"It's as if some men are yet to understand that, and with us living in a day and age where everything is far removed from where it is supposed to be, not only have we learned some behavioural traits that are wrong, but we have continued to practice them while also improving on them; efforts that have all led to where we are now; a place where it is common for men to believe that women should be satisfied with them making love as if they are at war or carrying feelings."

'Nuh likkle romance jus so-so…so?'

"I know all this might sound a way, but we have to face the facts. We live in a culture where being dominant is *ultimate; supreme,* and it doesn't matter what we are doing, as long as we are doing it, even if it is dealing with children, it's as if we just cannot help being dominant, and that dominance comes across in our relationships and even our sexual behaviour."

"This is what we live, see, hear, duplicate and then eventually pass on, all the time missing the point that although we live in a culture that says a man must have stamina to lay down the agony, if that's all he is bringing to the bedroom or wherever the escapade is going down, nine times out of ten, he is going to come up short. He may get his and feel like a champ, but miss the bigger picture all together, because if the performance wasn't anything to think about, or anything desirous of repeating, getting anymore is going to be a problem."

"It's just that simple, why allow yourself to be punished without reward, which is what most men are dishing out – punishment over pleasure."

69

Music is going to teach them a lesson

"Like I said earlier, I am no expert on this subject, because the entire subject of sex is very tricky in today's society, and what I find even funnier is how music gets blamed even in this area, especially here in Jamaica."

"Don't get me wrong now, because there are some songs that really go overboard, [TMI- Too Much Info], but even with that, I still find it kind of funny how the blame gets cast in the direction of music, or even how music got involved in such a conversation, because although music is very influential, saying music is to be blamed, or has contributed to promiscuity in society is still funny if we look at the bigger picture – none of what is going on is new, people were doing their thing way before what we now view as lewd or like we say in Jamaica, slackness, became popular."

"If we are going to be real, let's be real, because music wasn't always the scapegoat for promiscuity, but promiscuity had always been here, if it weren't so, relationships would've lasted and we wouldn't have so many dysfunctional and broken families today. I am not making any excuses for anybody, but things a gwaan long time, way before Punnany Rhythm, General Echo, Shabba Ranks and Vybz Kartel; music only highlights what is going on, it doesn't create it; at least not when it comes to this arena."

"So let's be real with this like with anything else, because just like poverty and oppression, which music didn't create either of, but music has always highlighted both of those negatives and other vices that plague our society, so why should music now take the blame for the

promiscuity in society, when dem ting dey a gwaan way before we even had the opportunity to hold a microphone?"

"I am a musician, so my opinion can be considered biased to some extent, but like I said, let's be real, things have been outta sync for as long as we have known them. And people can say whatever they want, but nothing can be hidden from this new generation, because once upon a time there was

Barry White
Soul Seduction

the innocent and those that weren't so innocent, but today all that have changed – everything is in the open."

"And again, let's not forget that all that we are talking about is old school anyway, none of this is new - Marvin Gaye and

Barry White were known to make baby - making music, and remember that way back in the 70s, General Echo aka Ranking Slackness, had songs like *Bathroom Sex* and *Twelve Inches of Pleasure*, so I am not going to sit here and act like I am a granny and talk one bag a tings that only sound good, but in reality, don't make any sense, because none of what is going on is new, it may just have more outlets to be heard, but it's not new by a long shot."

"What we also need to remember, is that musicians and entertainers are like the voice of the people, reporting, or highlighting issues on their behalf, and like it or not, sex is one of those issues, just like money."
"We have to keep in mind also that it is the people who build artistes or break them, so when an artiste like Pamputtae comes along and do her thing, if the people weren't with it, then she couldn't exist as an artiste, so that alone goes to show that like it or not, the masses relate and endorse the whole topic of sex in the Dancehall, in one way or the other."

"Think about it for a minute, if the topic of sex, whether

directly or indirectly, wasn't entwined somewhere in a song like Tony Matterhorn's *Dutty Wine,* do you think it would have been the sensation it was?...The answer is no, and the same is true for songs like *Bun Him* and *Dun Already.* The public is extremely interested in the topic of sex, in a variety of ways, shapes and forms – some may not like it for whatever reason, but that is why choice is important, because they don't have to listen to it, or attend the functions where these songs are played, but that does not mean that others don't want to hear them."

"Do I believe we artistes have a responsibility when it comes to the material that we put out, sexually explicit or otherwise?...Of course I believe we do, and the truth is some of us need to tone it down a bit, because things have changed so much where what we say and do is no longer confined to a nightclub or a dancehall environment, and young people, even more than adults are listening, and at the same time, they (young people) are looking up to us, so yes we have to be very careful and act responsibly, but we cannot be held responsible or be listed at the top of the list of contributing factors to moral decay: - what about families, what about individual responsibility, what about society at large, what about Hollywood? – The blame can be tossed far and wide, but that does not take away the fact that individually, we have to become more accountable."

"Like I said earlier, the entire subject of sex is tricky, because an artiste can always claim the right to artistic freedom, and he or she would be right, but the line still remains a thin and easy one to cross...Look at Jay-Z for example, in his book Decoded, he confesses to regretting the lyrics of his song, *'Big Pimpin.'* This is what Jay-Z said in a *Wall Street Journal*

interview, when asked about the lyrical content of the song: *"It was like, I can't believe I said that. And kept saying it. What kind of animal would say this sort of thing? Reading it was harsh."*....The Jay-Z example just goes to show how things can change, because truth is, that's how he felt when he did the song, but now all that has changed, society has changed, his views have changed and he now regrets it. And

73

he is not alone either, because I am sure if you ask some of our Dancehall artistes about some of their older material, they too might have some regrets here or there – and all this should be an example to be more conscious of what we are saying and how it might be viewed by others and even affect us in the future."

"It's a tricky one, but yes, we as artistes have to be more responsible, especially with a topic as sensitive as sex, but even with that, one thing is for sure, society's love affair with sex and sexual content of a variety of sorts is not going anywhere, anytime soon. Of course there is a problem in today's society with sexual practices and sexual activities, but it's not as simple as the powers that be would want us to believe it is, it's much more complex, and at the same time, let's not forget that sex is a very relevant subject, so we can be sure that it won't be off the Dancehall hot topic list anytime soon…..And in addition to all that, let's also keep in mind that Dancehall is an adult environment, and it's not the responsibility of any Dancehall or Reggae artiste to train up children, just as how it isn't the responsibility of any actor or actress to act as guardians; that is the responsibility of parents. Entertainers entertain, and they entertain their fans, and as long as their fans remain responsive and supportive, artistes are going to be writing, recording and performing lyrics with sexually explicit content. – That's just the way it is, just like Hollywood, as long as action movies sell, they are going to keep making them, each one going where the other didn't even think about going."

Bottom-line

"Sex is here to stay. It was here from creation, and it is always going to be here. If it wasn't for sex none of us would even be here to begin with, and if it isn't for sex, the replenishing of people would cease, so we have to deal with the realities. Sex is a wonderful and exciting thing, we all like it, like to do it, like to talk about it, some people even like to watch it, that's just how widespread and interesting it is, so much that it can even be addictive, and that alone makes it impossible for us to blame any one person or group for the behaviour of others, because we are all responsible for our own decisions and actions; even if there is outside influence – which there always is, this is life - so with that, I believe the solution is not a matter of saying who or what is to be blamed for what has now become a problem, but instead, I believe the solution to our sexed-up society is education, and not education that stops at condoms and other contraceptives, but a real in-depth move to re-educate society on what sex should really be and be about, and the responsibilities that come with having sex. That's how I see it, not just point the finger, because the problem is way bigger than we are even willing to admit."

"It would be nice to say, everyone should abstain from sexual activity until they are married, and then when they do get married, stick with their partner until death do they part. That would be nice, but as we are all quite aware, that's just not the way it works in today's society, so instead of talking around the problem and casting the blame on each other, for a problem that was here way before we even got here, [*people have been doing their cheating thing from way back – been having a whole lot of sneaking sex - babies have been having babies – none of this is new*] and since all this is true, why not try a different approach, because so far, all we seem to be doing is talk around the problem, and fail to realize that it is bigger than what we are talking about, with an even bigger reality to face....we are all wired for sex! God made us like that, so it is as natural as walking. The only difference is, from an early age we learn that certain places we simply do not walk, and I believe the same is true for sex; the training has to start from early if there is to be any resolve. It has to start early, not when children are teenagers, by then they are already curious, in experimental mode, and with hormones kicking, the thing can really get tricky if they are not educated properly – which is what I believe is the biggest problem in this arena – a lack of education, and this too, like anything to do with a child - which ultimately affects their future, in one way or the other - starts at home; - if not there, then where?"

The Doctor is in The House

Me & Beenie Man - We look good, don't?

Macka Diamond
&
Carlene [The ORIGINAL Dancehall Queen]

Macka
&
Black-Er - [Bun Him!!!]

Macka Diamond
&
Collie Buddz

Macka
&
R&B Crooner - Billy Ocean

79

Me & Machel Montano.......Soca King

In the company of intellects:

Me, Dr. Carolyn Cooper
&
Dr. Leahcim Semaj

Launch of -
The Real Gangster's Wife...

BBC interview after Sumfest perfromance 08

RE TV Interview after winning TWO -Teenage Observer Awards

Big Man Ting…

Me & Danny Champagne

STRAPPED!!!....Me & Mr. Renato Adams....

Me & Goddy-Goddy [Reggae Gospel Recording Artiste]

My fans come in all colours, shapes and nationalities

Me & Gueen Ifrica

Me & Patrice Roberts

Me & Mavado
doing the gully wine
in
NYC

Me
&
Nadine Sutherland

Every King fi have a Queen...
King Shango & Queen Macka

Dutty Link up - Me & Sean Paul

Me & Mr. Vegas

Me & the Governor
Lt. Stitchie

Me & The Big Belly One - Sky Juice

Me & some fans in Virgina - Book Tour

Me & Rita Marley - Di Real Mumma fi di ting...

Busted!

Nah...just me and some fans in uniform....NYC

Bad gal link up...

Me & Cecile in Trinidad

Sumfest 07

Being an artiste is way more than being on stage...believe that...

Me & Wayne Wonder after Celebrity Football Match in Miami

Nah sell out mi fren dem...

Me, Lady Ann [back in the day] -
Queen Paula & Lady G

Me - Marcia Griffiths
&
Morgan Heritage

Hot gal a road!!!!

Me & D'Angel in NYC

Me, The Mighty Sparrow & his wife

Me, Jam 2 & Lady G

Bun Him Book Launch - Florida

Me -& Oneil from Voicemail

ne But Not Forgotten

R.I.P.

Me -& Sugar Minott

Me & Minister Olivia Babsy Grange - [Min. Youth & Culture]

40 Things Every Woman Should Know......

Life has thought me a lot of lessons, and the more I live, the more I realize that it is so true when they say, *the more things change, the more they stay the same*...because we might have gotten more advanced technologically, not to mention more fabulous, and more

conscious about fashion and health than we have ever been, but when it comes to simple life skills, it's as if we have not made one step forward since I was a teenager..."

"I know that may sound as if I am demeaning the achievements of the entire human race, but on the contrary, I am not, and although what I say might not be the reality that you live, see or may even be familiar with, that does not make the reality I am addressing any less real, because it is a very real *reality*, in what I can almost say is literally my day to day experiences. The mistakes, social and otherwise of the past, are still being repeated in our present, with the saddest part of all being, the end result of such actions today being even greater than it was, let's say just a mere ten years ago."

"Like I said, a lot has changed, but just like yesterday or yesteryear; a lot still remains the same. And then to make it even more interesting, mistakes aside, I also find that a lot of things which I got right from early, things which have worked

101

and are still working to my benefit, a lot of women my age and even older, still have not gotten right yet, so it is with that mindset that I have put these vital lessons together, with the hope that it will not only come across as interesting, but do what I would love to do one on one with anyone who is willing to listen, put them up on game...Because that's all life is at times, a game....A game with winners and losers, and depending on how you play it, how you approach it, how you perceive it and all that other good stuff, it can either make you, break you or frustrate you – and with that said, I hope that these pointers help you as much as they have helped me.

Blessings

Macka

1. **God first, God second and God third:-** This is the first thing I think every woman should be aware of, because we can do nothing in our own strength and abilities, and it is my belief that without God, nothing is possible, so with that I say this, regardless who you are, what you have achieved, aim to achieve or what has happened to you, put God first in all your dealings – it's as simple as that – no explanation, no double talk.

2. **The best form of independence is financial; make sure you are saving some money every chance you get, you are going to need it: -** ...I guess some people are going to say money being at the top of my list is natural or expected, but they can say what they want to say, my Bible tells me clearly in Ecclesiastes chapter 10 verse 19 that, *'a feast is made for laughter, and wine makes merry; but money answers everything.'* So if the good book makes it that clear, who am I to disagree? This is the real world, and we

are going to need money every step of the way, each and every day. Regardless where on the list we may find ourselves, we all need money, because everything that we need on a daily basis in this physical, materialistic world comes with a price. When I talk about money it is not because Macka loves money, but it's because I love what money does for me and it's still even more than that. It's because I have had the same bank account since High School, so I understood the principle of saving from early, and understood that the more I saved along the way, the better position it would put me in, in the future. So with that said, this is a vital lesson I believe every female should be aware of; because like it or not, we live in a materialistic world, where money can work wonders for you, work wonders around you, or work wonders on you; so the decision is yours, but regardless of the decision you make, the reality remains the same – you are going to need money, so if the opportunity arises for you to save some, do so with enthusiasm, because you are going to need all you can get in the future – more later than now.

3. **All that glitters is not gold, and I'm not talking about jewelry either: -** ...I am talking about men, yes, men. As women we all tend to have these grand ideas of what our Mr. Right should be like, but ladies, take my advice, be very careful what you view as *Right*, because most times what we think is *Right*, has a funny way of eventually taking off their mask to reveal just how wrong they really are...This is not to say that all men turn out to be bad, but what I have found out from even my own experience, is that most do, and since that is the reality we have to face, it only makes sense that we invite caution to be a chaperone, because we have to be careful. Let's not be naive, anybody can act all nice and decent for a

while, but if they are not, believe me, the charade is going to end; it never fails. So ladies, don't be fooled or overwhelmed with how things are in the beginning when a member of the opposite sex shows interest in you, because relationships are not sprints, they are more like marathons, so pace yourself, don't use up all your energy in the beginning, nor don't allow yourself to be overwhelmed by all the attention that is shown in the early stages of a relationship, because all that is normal, *we all behave good at first- on the job, at school, wherever, that's just normal, human nature, especially if we are after something,* so don't be fooled, but be more impressed if his good qualities last beyond the first month or two...And a next important fact to note is don't be impressed by appearances, because just as we have knock-off or bootleg clothes and CDs/DVDs, we also also have knock-off and bootleg men, who appear to be one thing, but after one wash, or the moment you put them in the DVD player, it soon becomes clear that what they appeared to be could be nothing further from the truth. Cars, clothes, houses, name it, everything can be borrowed today, and some people have some unofficial keep and care jobs that come with all types of perks, and they know how to use them well; so again, be careful, because all that glitters is not gold.

SPECIAL NOTE: A man with real money never flaunts it in petty ways like on clothes, cars, jewelry and partying – so think about it, and after you do, take my advice, don't believe the hype, instead, put it to the test. *Don't mek dem fool unuh, mek dem put dem money wey dem mouth dey...Talk is cheap, and so is clothes and fake accessories.*

4. **Know what you want and how to get it from early:-** ....*A woman without a plan is already planning to fail.* This is another one of those philosophies that I learned from early on in life. I realized from early that I had to have a plan, and whatever decision I made, I had to stick to it. I realized that and I live by that until this day. We all get one shot at life, and very few of us get a second chance to get it right, so it only makes sense that we make every effort to get it right from early, or get it right the first time around, since there is no guarantee of a second. Very few people have more than one career in life, they may have more than one hustle, but a career is a lifelong process and that's not something that you decide in your thirties, you have to at least know what you are about by time you are in your twenties. Sure you can decide later, but since we only live once, it makes sense to me that we decide early and get the most out of our decision. I decided even before I was done with High School what I was going to do, and I have done it and always have, and if you don't want to use me as an example, then use any other successful female, and trust me, you're going to find out that she decided a long time ago what she was going to do with her life and perused it...This is life, and if you don't know what to do for yourself, or with your life, trust me, someone else will know exactly what to tell you to do, and know exactly where to direct or lead you to, and we all know how that can work out. We all have our own lives to live, and it is foolish to let someone else live yours or live yours the way they decide yours should be lived, but you have to know what you want, where you are going, and how you plan to get there; for some it might be school, and for some it might be some other type of hands-on training, but whatever it is, one thing is for sure, the earlier you figure out where you are going, the quicker you will get there, because you

would have made one vital step closer to your desire; a step that has nothing to do with age, but more so with self-awareness.

5. **Hope for the best, but expect the worst / What you give is not always going to be what you get:-**
This is one of those sad realities that I wish wasn't so, but sadly it is, and throughout life, regardless of who we are and what you or I are into, be it relationships, business, family matters or just everyday life, this is one reality that no woman should ever forget, because it never fails... Disappointment is always lurking in the shadows; so it's either you avoid the shadows or keep the lights on...It's as simple as that...As women we are often times more fragile emotionally than our male counterparts; things affect us differently, most times even deeper than they would affect a man; and with people, situations, circumstances, and life in general coming with so many disappointments, it again makes sense that we exert some level of caution and not allow our hearts and emotions to be shattered and trampled by expecting too much, or investing too much with the hope of reaping a harvest which never comes to fruition. If it works out differently for you then great, you are one of the lucky few, but check the ratio and see which category you are more likely to fall in...So let's be real and not fool ourselves, if life has dealt you one of those great hands, then great, but don't fool yourself and act as if it's all good, and walk around with your head in the cloud...Do not be naïve and always expect things to just work out as if you are special, because when it comes to disappointment, none of us are exempt. I am sorry to disappoint you if no one ever told you any of this before, but don't kill the messenger, this is life, real life, and most times,

the disappointments often times outweigh the expected satisfactions, hopes and even dreams that we hold dear...Sure we have to live, and sure if disappointment comes it comes, but how we prepare for those inevitable moments makes all the difference; the difference between getting up and dusting ourselves off and moving on, and laying on the ground defeated, feeling sorry for ourselves.

6. **Everybody has a brain, use yours for yourself and stop depending on others to use theirs for you, and while you are thinking about that, make sure you don't allow someone else to use yours [your brain] for you:-** Have you ever noticed that everyone always has some great advice to give you on whatever it is that you are dealing with or going through'?...Think about it, if they know so much, why haven't they done it, or why aren't they doing it? My Grandmother always sey, *'mouth cut cross way mek fi sey anyting,'* which simply means anyone, can say whatever, as long as they have a mouth. It is as simple as that, and I have come to realize that most people just like to hear themselves talk, or like to appear as if they have some type of knowledge that you don't; like their brain is in perfect working order and yours isn't. Well this is my take on that matter, God gave all of us a brain, just like He gave us hands, feet and eyes, and we use them individually, to touch, walk and to look at what we want, when we want and how we want, and I am convinced that the same is true for the brain...God gave us all one brain, all with the same capabilities, so use yours and stop letting others use yours for you, or use theirs for you.

7. **Most things are for the moment, temporary distractions; don't be fooled, the picture is always bigger than what it appears to be; understand**

what really matters and what doesn't:- As long as we are alive there is always going to be something that is being marketed to us that we feel as if we just cannot do without and just have to have. This can be anything from clothes, cars, handbags, shoes, just name it, but what many women do not know, is that this is one of the main areas in their lives where they are either defeated, distracted or worse, experience major set backs...Ladies, what was the fashion craze last summer?.... Most might not even remember, and for those who do, how much did you spend on it, and guess what, there is something new this summer, something new this winter, this spring and this fall. That's just the way it is, there is always going to be something new, because the people who make these items are into the business of making stuff for us to buy; and nothing is wrong with that. What however is wrong, is when we allow these trends that change so often to dictate how we spend what we earn; all of which amounts to nothing much after you wear the outfit a couple of times, and with the way things are moving, by the time you are ready to wear it again, it may be outdated. So what was it for, why spend on it like we do, when most of us are not in the position to do it anyway, and then to make it worse, the investment is so fleeting, it's outdated as soon as you buy it?

Remember the Burberry Plaid craze a few years ago, and before that what was it, D&G?...Remember Tommy Hilfiger and FUBU, yea, they came and we spent, and they left richer than they came, and we were left with a whole bunch of stuff that didn't take long to not matter anymore. Today there seems to be a Gucci and Louis Vuitton craze, and just like all those brands before, they too will fade from the spotlight, replaced by something that is more hip and trendy. It never fails, we can go all the way back to the Bell-

Bottoms and Platforms of the 70s, so my point is clear, some things are just for the moment, and to move forward, we must be wise in even these areas that so many of us seem to take for granted...Just think about if for a minute, if all we do is follow the next so called *hot thing,* without even realizing it in no time we'll find ourselves working or hustling just for merchants, and at the end of the day, left with all this stuff that we nor anybody else wants.

BOTTOMLINE: Looking good is a must, but not every trend is for you, me or her, especially if it takes money from us that could be used for something more lasting and substantial.

8. **Figuring out your life is your responsibility, and If you don't believe in yourself along the way, no one else will:-** Life is like a jigsaw puzzle, and we all have our own to figure out. The pieces are all around, but you have to find them and put it together. Don't expect too much help along the way either, because everyone you meet has the same task, and even if they have theirs figured out already, it's still best to put yours together yourself – I mean, who has your interest at heart more than you?

9. **Never drop your initial standard:-** First impressions last, and they last in more ways than one, and also affecting how you are dealt with along the way. Whether it's relationships or business, your first impression will last, and it is the standard by which you will be dealt with from there on out. Keep your standard high, and never lower it, because the minute you do, is the minute the ground of respect that you were standing on is moved from under you...Believe it or not, we- you / me, dictate to others how they deal with us by how we carry ourselves, and if they see

109

that our standards are low, then that's how they will deal with us, but if your standards are of a totally opposite nature, then they have no choice but to deal with you accordingly. Sure people will try, they will test you, but that's life – you, me, we all do the same thing if we can, but it's on us to maintain our standards and not compromise, because the moment we do, that is the moment all hope of respect is lost.

10. **Education is still key:-** I may be an entertainer, but I finished High School. I could've dropped out and started hanging out at studios but I didn't, why? Because I realized from early that talent alone will not make it in this industry, that industry or life in general. A person with no literate ability will always have a problem in this world, there is just no way around it, you have to have some educational foundation, regardless how simple it is, if it's even the basics. The truth is, life today really requires much more than that, but with that at least you have a foundation to build on, which is vital, because if you don't have even that, then you really have nothing – Some of us didn't get the chance to do all we could've done in school, due to whatever circumstances, but keep in mind that it's never too late to get it right, as long as there is life, there is hope, and never let pride hold you back either, people are always going to talk, but talk is cheap, plus none of what they say will matter after you get it right anyway – believe that!

11. **Don't put off for tomorrow what you can do today:-** Procrastination is one of our biggest stumbling blocks along the journey of life, but what we need to remember is that tomorrow is promised to no man or woman, and each day brings its own opportunities and yes, its own disappointments, but regardless, why not make the most of today. Sure you

may be able to do tomorrow what you could have done today, but what if tomorrow comes and you cannot do it for whatever reason?... In other words, if you have it to do today, and you can get it done today...*do it!*...Don't let it wait, because not only isn't tomorrow promised, life and time waits for no man or woman...**REMEMBER**: Tomorrow will always come with its challenges and disappointments, so deal with today, today.

12. **Come clean early, surprises don't add much value to relationships:-** We all have our little secrets, or what we think are secrets, but if anyone else knows, then I am sorry to be the bearer of bad news, but what you think is your little secret, is no longer a secret anymore, and if what they know could affect a relationship, be it personal, family or business, it's best if you were the first one to bring such sensitive information to light, if for one second you believe It may eventually find its way to the surface with a few negative connotations attached, which is usually the case when told by someone who isn't too fond of you.

13. **Sometimes it's best to keep your opinions to yourself:-** My grandmother would say, *"Is not everyting good fi eat, good fi talk,"* which simply means; It's not everything that you know you should tell. Most of us have heard this before, but some of us need to say it over and over again until we remember it and then apply it, because as women we always seem to be getting into some, *he says-she says* crap, and except when someone is outright lying, most of what some of us find ourselves in is no fault of anyone but ourselves, because if we never said anything to begin with, then no one could twist what we had said, or say we said when we didn't

111

say…Sometimes what you say may be the truth, but you know what they say about the truth…*it hurts*… And we all know people don't react too kindly to pain…So if you ask me, sometimes it's good not to have an opinion, at least not vocally.

14. **Men like what they see in the beginning, and they don't change much along the way; ladies, don't get too comfortable and let yourself go after you feel you have met Mr. Right:-** There is a big misconception that when a woman has a man it's time to relax and enjoy the ride. Well, that may be true for a while, but after the honeymoon fades, it's time to put in work, because just as he saw you, he will see someone else if you aren't worth looking at anymore…Sure relationships are about way more than looks and appearances, but let's be real, isn't that where and how 99% of them start?

15. **Live within your means:-** It's nice to admire all the different things that we don't have and would like to have, but if you can't afford it, for your own good, leave it alone! Putting your hat where you can't reach it will either lead to the need of a ladder or jumping to get it, and both could lead to an accident, so why risk the danger and embarrassment?…Which is exactly what living outside of your means will do to you.

16. **Fake it until you make it:-** Don't get it twisted, I am not talking about faking overall, but I do believe that the only thing you should be faking is confidence. If you don't have it yet, pretend you do. In every new situation, pretend you're not nervous, pretend you're not afraid. After a few times doing this, the pretence disappears, so much that you may even start convincing yourself.

17. **When you say goodbye, let go and move on:-** Ladies, well maybe not you, but most of us seem to have an issue with letting go, and this doesn't only stop at intimate relationships either, it goes for all areas of our lives. We all get attached to things and people, and when things go wrong we tend to hold on for dear life, overlook, forgive and forget, name it and some of us have done it, all the time overlooking the fact that we have just set ourselves up for a repeat of a lot more of the same. Letting go hurts, but holding on after being hurt, can eventually hurt much more.

18. **It's alright to make a mistake once, maybe even twice, but if you keep making the same mistake over and over again, it's no longer a mistake, it's a habit:-** The same effort and circumstances will always bring about the same results, and if it were a mistake the first time around, it's going to be a mistake the second and third times around, even if it's in a different place, and with a different person, but as long as the circumstances are the same or similar, the end results are always going to be the same or similar as before. Mistake then, mistake now and mistake later. Learn from them, don't repeat them.

19. **Don't be offended by opinions, we all have one, two, three, four and more, and sometimes they don't amount to much:-** People are going to say what they want, whether it's true, or not, and whether they know what they are talking about or not, but it's on you to not allow what they say [opinions of others] to dictate your reality.

20. **When the going gets tough, the tough gets going:-** We have all heard that before, but how many of us realize how real it is. Well just so you know, it is, because when things get tough, it's either you

toughen up and deal with them, or let them beat you down and keep you down...The choice is yours – always yours - regardless of the situation or circumstance.

21. **Never get too busy for those that really matter:-** While pursuing dreams and careers, at times we tend to develop a severe case of tunnel vision, which we disguise as focus, but keep this in mind, your job or dream won't take care of you when you are sick or need that compassionate hand, but your friends, family and parents will. Stay in touch.

22. **Even when you know you are right, you will not and won't win every argument. Agree to disagree:-** Sometimes it's best to let some things slide, especially if you see that the conversation is going nowhere; save your energy for more civil exchanges, not everyone is open to reason, even if it makes all the sense in the world.

23. **Stop comparing your life to others. You have no idea what is really going on behind what you can see:-** What you see isn't always what it is, and although another person's life may look wonderful from where you are standing, it just may surprise you how things really are if you were to get a glimpse of what things are really like behind the scene. Like Bob said, *'if night could turn to day, a lot of people would run away.'*

24. **Ladies, if you are not wanted, meaning you are not a fugitive from the law, don't allow anybody to hide you:-** This one is simple, if you are with a man and he has to keep you on the down low, it's time to go. It's that simple, night nurses have day

appearances too, and even pin cushions get used in the light of day.

25. **Whatever doesn't kill you really does make you stronger, but it is also suppose to make you wiser:-** Stronger is good, but wiser is always better. It's always better to learn from the mistakes of others, but if you have to learn from your own, make sure you are in class...Brains outweigh muscles any day – stronger yes, but wiser is always better.

26. **Special occasions depend on you, not just a date on the calendar:-** Get away, act like you have just met are in love all over again and again, do it every chance you get. Light some candles, bring out the nice sheets, bring out the sexy lingerie, and if you don't have any, get some. Live your life and enjoy it to the fullest. Don't save it for a special occasion. Today is as special as any.

27. **Nothing lasts forever – it's true, so this too [whatever it is] will pass:-** Another one of those old lessons I learned from early, and a lesson that has proven itself to be true, time and time again. Unpleasant things will happen, this is life, but regardless how bad a situation is, or how deep the wound is, it will not only change, but time heals all wounds – what's done is done, let go and live, remember now, we only live once.

28. **Growing old beats dying young any day:-** Wouldn't you agree?...I thought so...Ladies, never let talk of your age affect you in any way, shape or form, because the reality is this, as long as we keep waking up, we are all going to get older, like it or not!...Let's just be glad we are alive and stop complaining, or allow ourselves to be affected by what others have to

say while they are getting older as they talk without even realizing it.

29. **Small minds talk about people, average minds talk about events, greats minds create the events the average minds talk about:-** Nobody knows better than you where you fall in this category – check yourself.

30. **When in doubt, step back / avoid it, put it off, do whatever you have to do, but don't proceed if there is any doubt:-** We have all made the mistake of getting into something or doing something that we weren't so sure of to begin with, and sometimes, most times if we were to be honest, such actions bring about results that are not so pleasant, so why keep doing it? – When in doubt, step back / avoid it – it's that simple; better to be safe than sorry. A pound of prevention is better than an ounce of cure.

31. **We have all asked and may all ask again, but there is never an answer to the question of, *why*?:-** Deal with whatever it is and move on, asking *why* is never going to change it, even if you do get an answer; what's done is done.

32. **There is only one of you, and after you, there won't be another you:-** God made one of all of us, and He did it for a reason, so why go against His will and try to be someone else...Admire them - yes, but be the best you there is, not just another them.

33. **Where you are tomorrow depends on what you do today:-** For years people have talked about wanting to rule their own destinies, but fail to realize that they, we, are already all in charge of our own destinies, regardless of our circumstances – some may

116

disagree, but like it or not, every living moment is setting the stage for the next, and you are always in control – again, circumstances making no difference whatsoever – because what you are dealing with is what you are dealing with, and what you decide in that situation dictates the next – it's that simple.

34. **As good as you may be at what you do, you are not the first to do it that well, and believe it or not, there is always someone better:-** Humility is key - Sometimes we all get ahead of ourselves, and it takes a big woman to step back and know that she is still in control – because if you are as good at whatever it is that you claim to be so good at, then the proof is in the pudding, just do it, if it's all that, it will be seen – be about it, don't just talk about it and flaunt it- let whatever it is be seen – actions still do speak louder than words - and attitude without altitude is loony – *it nuh look good* - real talk – if you're di shit, trust me, they will smell you.

35. **The world is bigger than what you have seen, heard of or know about:-** Different strokes for different folks, like it or not that's just the way it is, and as long as we are alive, we will either have to accept it or be agitated by it. What we believe is right is what we believe is right, (and I am not talking about legalities) but in the same breath, what we believe is right, may not be considered right to someone else, and it goes the other way around also…I have been to many places and some of the customs are different, way different from what I am used to at home, but I can't go there and act as if I want to change the people's way of doing things in a few days, when they have been doing what they have been doing for God He knows how long – Sometimes

117

we allow our egos and shallow perceptions of life to blind us.

36. **Change with the times, but don't let the times change you:-** What you have already learned is great, but there are always new things to learn. Life is a constant work in progress, and since you are reading this, I guess it's safe to assume that you are amongst the living, which simply means that you, like life, is also a work in progress – in other words, don't get stuck in an era, move with it, evolve, grow, get familiar with new technology, get used to the new way of doing the same old thing; don't sound bitter talking about back in your day – this isn't back in your day, this is today, and things have changed – get used to it – they don't have to change you, but to keep progressing, like it or not you will have to adjust, even if it's just a bit.

37. **There still isn't any such thing as a stupid question:-** If you don't know something - ask, it's that simple. Who cares what someone has to say about you after you have gotten the information that you were seeking? – And what makes more sense, asking and being looked at in a funny way, or acting like you know something and then end up looking like a dummy? – Questions were made to be asked – so ask.

38. **Communication is a vital part of any relationship:-** A lot of couples didn't get the memo that said, the longer they are together, the closer they are suppose to become, and instead of drawing closer with time, they drift apart for whatever reason. Communication is never always the problem, but most times it's the solution, and communication does not mean arguing either – Forget what you have seen on TV, there are

no mind readers, and that goes for your companion, business associates, family members, friends, whoever. No one reads minds, and unless you open your mouth and let what's on your mind be known, no one will know what you are thinking or feeling and if they don't know, how can they even begin to address what you are thinking or feeling, in an appropriate manner? – If you don't talk, no one will hear you, and if you can't talk, write it, use hand signals, do something, but whatever you do, communicate.

39. **Ladies, never assume that you know what a man likes or doesn't like [in bed or out of bed] without asking him, what he likes may just surprise you:-** This is where it gets interestingly tricky, because as similar as all men are, they are also different in their own way. They like different things, and they like them done a certain way, and if your aim is to please, then it only makes sense that you ask most women don't, and this is what makes asking him to basically instruct you so seductive - Ask, and if you are too shy to ask, try different things, believe me, if you get it right he is going to let you know.

40. **The best is always yet to come:-** This is all about holding on to hope; a key ingredient in life, which if lost, leaves you with nothing – literally!.

Final thought: Sometimes as women we allow ourselves to become handicapped by our gender and a bunch of other things that really didn't matter, or don't add up after all that's said and done. There are some of us who act as if we're too fragile to do certain things, or act as if we shouldn't do them, period! All this may appear cute for a moment, but with time, believe me, it's going to lose its appeal, so don't just sit and act like a Barbie Doll all your life – being cute is nice, but things like being computer literate, being able to drive and even changing a tyre also matter, and oh, so do domestic matters, and just for the record, this has nothing to do with being a maid either, but instead, has everything to do with you being a woman in this ever changing fast-paced world – A world that is calling for way more than a pretty face these days.

Selah